Shanty Life on the
Settle-Carlisle Railway

A Revised Edition

Shanty Life on the Settle-Carlisle Railway

by W. R. Mitchell

CASTLEBERG

When the Midland Railway Company decided to drive a fast, all weather route from Settle to Carlisle in the 1870s, John Crossley (above) delayed his retirement as Chief Engineer so that he might surpervise the work. Local people were to recall "navvy time," when a 72 mile strip of land swarmed with workers. A viaduct such as Smardale (left) demanded skilled categories, including masons and carpenters. Long wooden huts, painted white to deflect the rays of the summer sun, housed families or stores. A group of huts stood at what is now Marshfield Road in Settle (below).

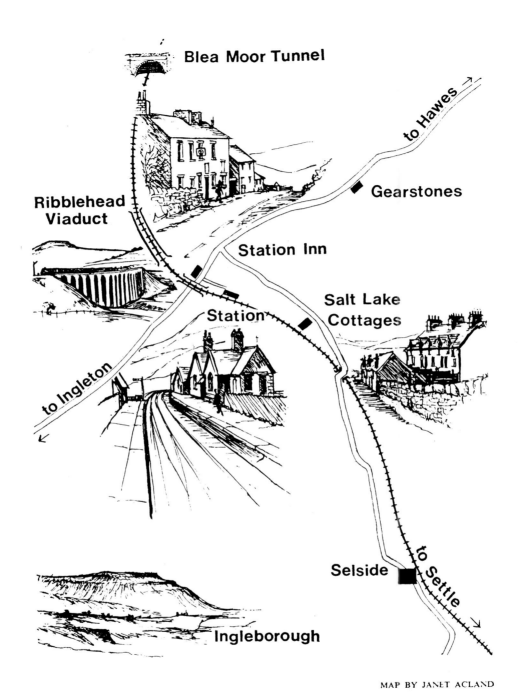

Blea Moor Tunnel

to Hawes

Gearstones

Ribblehead
Viaduct

Station Inn

Salt Lake
Cottages

Station

to Ingleton

to Settle

Selside

Ingleborough

MAP BY JANET ACLAND

Typeset and printed by Lamberts Print & Design, Station Road, Settle, North Yorkshire, BD24 9AA.
Published by W.R. Mitchell, 18 Yealand Avenue, Giggleswick, Settle, North Yorkshire, BD24 0AY.
© Text, W.R. Mitchell, 1988. Reprinted 1996. Revised edition 2004.
ISBN: 1 871064 01 5

A Railway Surveying Party.

Contents

Illustrations

Front Cover, top – Jack Foster, of Austwick, who was among those providing meat for the navvies (Author's Collection). *Left* – Settle Church prior to 1870 (Horner Collection). *Bottom* – Impression of Batty Green shanty town (Betty Harrington, courtesy of North Craven Building Trust).

Back Cover, top – Dent Head viaduct in course of construction (BR). *Bottom* – Group of miners at Nenthead. Their clothes and manner would be similar to those of the railway navvies on the nearby Settle-Carlisle.

Uncredited photographs by the author.

Page 1 (half title page) – Ribblehead viaduct, in course of construction (drawing, from Williams's history of the Midland Railway Company, 1878). The engraver based his drawing on a contemporary photograph.

Above – Sketch of railway surveyors at work (from Williams's "Our Iron Roads," 1852).

Drawings on pages 7, 13, 21, 31, and head and shoulders sketches of men are from the pen of Rowland Lindup.

Drawings on pages 10, 15 (top), 16 (top), 26 (top), 32, by Betty Harrington (courtesy of North Craven Building Trust).

Map on page 12 by Nigel Mussett.

Foreword by Brian Sutcliffe

**(Former Chairman
of the Friends of
the Settle-Carlisle
Line Association)**

Below: North Portal, Blea Moor Tunnel.

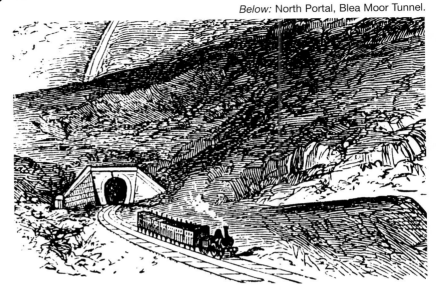

I FIRST became acquainted with the Settle to Carlisle Railway in the mid-1960s, little knowing that 15 years later I was to become actively involved in a fight to save the line from closure. My first impressions were of the stark beauty of the landscape and the characterful viaducts and tunnels as the line carved its way through the Pennine hills before entering the lush Eden valley for the latter part of its journey to Carlisle.

I travelled in the front coach of the all-stations Skipton to Carlisle DMU. As the train passed Ais Gill summit I saw, in the distance and far below, a plume of smoke. It was outlined against the hillside. As the trains converged, a Class 9F came into view blasting smoke skywards as it struggled to haul its rake of loaded anhydrite wagons to the summit.

This was the epitome of the line in the twilight area of steam and many books have sought to perpetuate that image. Within a few years, steam had disappeared, as had the local service. The line had entered a period of decline which culminated in an announcement about closure. That is when I became involved. Dramatic changes have since taken place; the Settle-Carlisle continues to meet the needs of passengers and those concerned with freight.

How many of these passengers even consider how the line was constructed? It was built towards the end of the railway mania, over a century ago, when inter-company rivalries and politics forced the Midland Railway to make a line that in the end they never really wanted. The Settle-Carlisle was the last main line to be constructed by traditional "navvy methods". In writing this foreword, I recognise the achievement of the thousands of navvies who worked on the project.

Having spent five years battling, with others, to save the line from closure, I can appreciate something of the effort of the navvies who spent five years battling to build Ribblehead. They must have been special people indeed, to tolerate the vagaries of the Pennine weather which, at times, would make living and working conditions a nightmare.

No traces remain of the shanty towns that were home to many people. There are reminders in local churches and churchyards of those who gave their lives during the construction of a masterpiece of Victorian civil engineering. The greatest memorial is the railway, with its viaducts and tunnels. Let us hope that passengers can continue to enjoy for many more years the very special experience offered by the Settle to Carlisle railway.

An impression of a Railway Shanty.

Memories of "Navvy Time"

MY INTEREST in shanty towns began in the 1950s, when I saw a harmonium in the waiting room at Ribblehead station, on the Yorkshire Pennines. The room was still being used for Sunday worship. I discovered that in "navvy time", the 1870s, hundreds of people lived in wooden huts that were grouped all the way from the road to the summit of Blea Moor. The Midland, anxious to pacify as well as Christianise its cosmopolitan labour force, appointed a Scripture Reader for the area; the contractor built him a mission room where services might take place.

When the railway was opened; when the hutments had been disbanded and cleansing Pennine winds swept away all traces of the shanty life, the local people obtained permission to hold services at the new station. In the 1930s, the harmonium was being used to accompany the hymn-singing. Someone described this wheezy instrument as an "ill wind that nobody blows any good"!

At the nearby Salt Lake Cottages, I was shown a desk used when the workmen at Batty Green were being paid. Behind the wine store at Settle stood a wooden hut that was said to have been part of a "canteen" from Ribblehead, bought at the Midland Company's sale of unwanted material. It is possible the hut was once owned by Messrs Burgoyne and Cocks, shopkeepers and large-scale bakers. In conversation with the Preston family I heard of grandfather's role of nipper, or errand-boy for the railway engineers. He once took a message to Blea Moor and was allowed to descend a shaft to watch the miners at work.

Willie Preston told me of impoverished families who remained in the area when the work was done. Some of them lived for a while "under the arches" (those of Kirkgate viaduct) and they stretched tarpaulins across the void to cheat the weather. Years ago, a lad who had been given a metal-detector as a Christmas present asked me to take him to the area of the Ribblehead shanties. We concentrated on the conspicuous line of the tramway. The instrument "pinged" from time to time, but all we recovered were heavy bolts and a penny dropped during the construction period, as the date confirmed.

In 1976, when the Settle-Carlisle celebrated its centenary, I was on a small committee formed to arrange for some celebrations. Eventually, with the co-operation of British Railways, we celebrated in style when a train composed of vintage coaches drew up at Settle station and a meal was served in a marquee. There were speeches, too, including one imbued with evangelistic fervour, delivered by Bishop Treacy of Wakefield.

Nigel Mussett, Bill Brocklebank and myself researched the subject of the shanty towns to such good effect that we published a booklet and devised an exhibition. By now, we were familiar with the shanties – with Batty Wife Hole, Sebastopol, Inkerman, Jericho, Jerusalem and Tunnel Huts. And we knew of some of the more outrageous characters, such as Welsh Nobby, The Pincer, Leeds Polly, Devon Sam, Tiger, Gipsy, Dagger and Belter, not forgetting Policeman Jack, who slew William Williams in bare-fisted fighting on the Black Moss of Garsdale.

RECORDS testify to the marshy nature of the pre-railway Batty Green. A contemporary account tells of men walking home through the mire with a careless indifference to their well-being. Supplies such as bricks were transported by "bog cart," which consisted of a light cart-body, with a barrel that would revolve "like a gigantic garden roller." As many as three horses in a row hauled the cart over the softest areas.

Above: Ribblehead Viaduct and Batty Green (Photo: Peter Fox).
Below: A partly completed viaduct at Ormside, in Edenvale.

Mealtime in a navvy family's hut

How They Lived at the Moorland Hutments

IN THE autumn of 1869, the peace of Chapel-le-Dale was stirred by a traction engine that was hauling a four-wheeled van from Ingleton to Ribblehead. It was rumoured that the journey had begun in London. The van was brought to a halt beside the old turnpike between Lancaster and Richmond, near the place where it was joined by the Ribblesdale road. This is a wild spot. John Ruskin, travelling up the dale on a windy day, marvelled that the mountain Ingleborough could stand without rocking. The van, grandly known as The Contractor's Hotel, provided accommodation for engineers and their helpers.

The 1869-70 winter was long and severe and in the darkest weather a man stood at the door of the van and held up a bull's-eye lantern as a guide to his colleagues. The men who did the preliminary work on Blea Moor lived in tents and their supplies were delivered on the backs of donkeys.

By July, 1870, over 40 huts had been erected. The number grew steadily. The contractor soon realised that the large labour force would not be able to find lodgings in existing dwellings and so high priority was given to providing temporary accommodation. A typical hut was long enough to have three capacious sections, one as sleeping accommodation for the principal family, the second for the lodgers and the third to be used as a combined kitchen and dining area.

I have seen three photographs on which huts appear. One shows a group at Settle, in what is now Marshfield Road, near a recently completed viaduct, and – this being summer – the huts had been whitewashed to deflect the sun's glare. A second photograph, of Ribblehead, with a partly completed viaduct, clearly shows a group of huts, some with porches, which I believe represents Belgravia, a rather posh suburb of Batty Green. A third picture is, I think, of Dent Head (the photographic image was reversed in the printing). It was here, north of Blea Moor, that a settlement called "Six Huttes" was established.

The style of the contractor's hut, expressing "fitness for purpose", changed little over the years, until the arrival of portacabin (for the office) and private caravans (accommodating the men).

In the 1870s, most of the huts were well-kept and had a homely atmosphere. "The hardy wives of railway operatives decorated their wooden walls with paper hangings and pictures cut from illustrated newspapers and periodicals", wrote a visitor to the Ribblehead group in 1872. "They make substantial meals, keep good fires and study the comfort of their lodgers".

In 1874, Sedbergh's Medical Officer of Health was appalled by the overcrowding and unhygenic conditions he found at Denthead, where some of the huts had been set on bogland. He estimated that the cubic space for each occupant in the sleeping apartments was very much below 300 feet, "the minimum required for the maintenance of health."

In one hut he noticed five bedsteads jammed so tightly together "that the sleepers, in reaching the furthest beds, must necessarily clamber over the others." The huts, being on boggy ground, were approached on planks or stepping stones. There was "no vestage of drainage save the open trenches cut around the walls of the huts to protect them from inundation." No provision appeared to have been made for the separation of the sexes.

The 1871 census is our first detailed record of those who were living at the shanties of Ingleton Fells, as the area was known administratively. The entry for James Tiplady is of special interest. He is described as "home missionary," having been appointed in deliberations between the Midland Railway and the Bradford City Mission, to minister to the railway workers and their families on Contract No.1. Tiplady's dwelling was No.3 Batty Wife Hole and he is stated to be 26 years of age. His hut appears to have been capacious, for he had a lodger, 21 year-old Jane Herbert, from Essex, and – to observe Victorian convention – a servant lass, 16 year-old Eliza E. Combs. It would be unthinkable that the missionary should live under a single roof with a young spinster.

Their neighbours were, by and large, decent folk. The men would return home after work, wash and tidy themselves, sit down to a good savoury meal, and then read or form themselves into choral or instrumental groups.

It was left to a Methodist local preacher to visit the navvies in the remoter hutments. In 1872, such a man, with the co-operation of the Contractor, Mr Ashwell, travelled by horse and trap from Batty Green to Dent Head. "While passing the numerous huts one could not but notice the pigs, ducks and hens wandering at large on the moor, showing that the railway operatives, however unfavourably circumstanced, cannot rest without they are surrounded with the domestic animals." Another writer mentioned an infestation of rats; they had "jovial doings among the hut inhabitants" and were "much given to nightly rompings above the ceilings."

It is known that pedlars made the rounds of the upper shanties and on Saturday afternoon, the Market Train conveyed shoppers in open trucks to visit the shops at Batty Green. A newspaper writer of 1871 noted: "Though the hut villages of Batty Green, Sebastopol and Jericho are upon a dreary moor far away from the busy marts of commercial men, still there is no lack of roast beef, savoury pastry, luscious fruits and beveridges of pleasant flavour to lovers of the bottle."

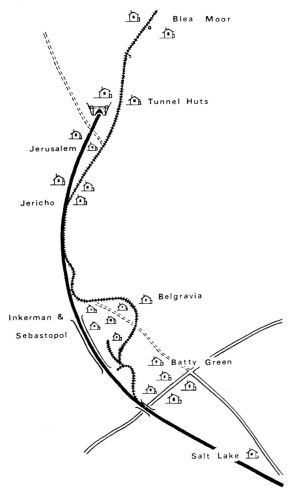

Blea Moor

Tunnel Huts

Jerusalem

Jericho

Belgravia

Inkerman &
Sebastopol

Batty Green

Salt Lake

The name most familiar to shoppers in "navvy time" was that of Messrs Burgoyne and Cocks – a name that varied in its spelling—who served Contract No.1. The partners had premises in Settle and Batty Green. From here they supplied smaller shops at Stainforth, Helwith Bridge, Horton, Selside, Ashes, Sebastopol, Jericho, Tunnel Huts and Dent Head. So successful were the two businessmen that in 1871, within a year of commencing to supply the railway families with provisions, the partners moved to new premises in Duke Street, Settle. "This establishment is a great improvement to the street, and on this account the firm last week gave their customers 500 glass cream jugs and sugar basins."

At Settle, using two large ovens, Messrs Burgoyne and Cocks produced 4,000 loaves of bread daily and nearby was a large "butching shop" where four fat cows and from 10 to 15 sheep, besides "porklings and fat pigs" were slaughtered weekly. The partners also catered for the minds of its customers, and from the Batty Green premises were distributed newspapers and periodicals.

Mr Cocks appears to have been the financial wizard. He pored over the books, and was quick to detect discrepancies, such as those occurring in the ledgers being kept by the manager at Helwith Bridge. Mr Cocks immediately instructed his partner to investigate, and to ensure that no further goods were taken until legal proceedings began. Messrs Burgoyne and Cocks lost £16 of goods through a derailment on the light railway extending from Batty Green to Blea Moor. An accident occurred, the last wagon plunging into a gorge. Pilferers took the partners' goods—half a fat cow, a fat sheep and other merchandise. Incidentally, we know that John Clark Garlic was an innkeeper and grocer at Batty Green because a navvy called Thomas Jones stole an oil lamp and five pieces of scented soap from his shop window.

In Black and White

Two documents from the period immediately before the construction of the Settle-Carlisle line.

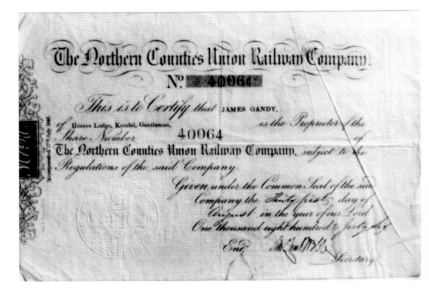

Above: A share certificate of The Northern Counties Union Railway Company, which consisted of a triumvirate that included a proposed Leeds & Carlisle railway (via Otley, Kirkby Stephen and Appleby, joining the Lancaster-Carlisle at Clifton, near Penrith).

Left: A Duplicate Conveyance dated July 19, 1870 between James Farrer, of the Ingleborough Hall Estate, and the Midland Railway Company. The document refers to land in the parishes of Horton-in-Ribblesdale, Bentham and Sedbergh.

A Tramway on to Blea Moor

Early priority was given to laying tracks for rail transport between Batty Green and the summit of Blea Moor. The tramway was used to move coal to the steam engines at the tunnel shafts. A Shoppers' Train from the high shanties to the shops of Ribblehead was organised each Saturday. *Above* – An impression of men laying the tramway; they were said to have "worked like Yankees." *Below* – A length of rail, found among rubble left on the Moor.

Above – An impression by Betty Harrington of life on Batty Green.

Below – Making an embankment in the old-fashioned way, with horses and carts. Hundreds of horses were needed on the course of the line.

Food for the Mind

BY DECEMBER, 1870, a capacious mission room stood at Batty Green. The plainness of the walls was off-set by "pictorial embellishment" intended to teach the virtues of thrift and kindness. Across one end of the room was a platform, with a rostrum at which the missionary, Mr Tiplady, might stand. Space was available for his gospel singers. The worshippers sat on forms with "backs" and the room was heated by large stoves. Mr Tiplady impressed all by his assiduous labours and the Revd W.M. Harper, of Chapel-le-Dale, was stated to be a man of genial spirit. In 1871, a wooden church was erected at Dent Head, to be served by Mr Tiplady. Such a building was known as a "mission station" and clergymen and lay preachers were encouraged to take services here. The Methodists emulated John Wesley and in summer held open-air services.

Mr Tiplady's mission room provided food for mind and body. In March, 1871, about 100 people attended a tea party. So much food was available that "large heaps of fragments were left." The idea of a day school at Batty Green was broached in August, 1870. It was opened in the springtime of 1871, when Miss Herbert of Nottingham had 43 scholars who were reported to be clean, neatly attired "and on account of their docility and good behaviour a credit to their parents and the railway public." Children from other shanty towns did not attend this school because of the distance they must walk and also on account of the poor state of the road. A visitor in October, 1871, noted that "groups of children here and there were sitting on the moor, which

must, on account of its swampy condition, be very injurious to their health. Surely the Midland Company might do something towards the education of those neglected children who through the circumstances of the workmen are deprived of the educational advantages of towns and villages."

It was at the school, in 1874, that a series of concerts took place to raise money for a tablet, to be placed in Chapel-le-Dale Church, "in remembrance of the poor workmen who have lost their lives by accident on the Settle-Carlisle railway." When it was announced that a concert would be followed by a grand ball, the demand was considerable and the dancers did not disperse until 6am. Another time, a concert was organised for the benefit of Leeds Infirmary; the seats were pricey but every seat was occupied. Messrs Burgoyne and Cocks returned yet more of the good profits they were making on the sale of provisions: they sponsored this event.

In typical Victorian fashion, the Midland Railway and its Contractor did their best to divert the mens' attention from "pursuits and places of a corrupting character." As early as 1871, Penny Readings were being held each week at Batty Green where, in due course, a Reading Room was opened "for mental improvement and social entertainment." A Penny Reading included songs as well as recitations. The idea was to expose the audience to the gamut of emotion, from sadness to elation, by varying the tone of the items. The size of the audience was related to the weather! The proceeds were sent to a worthy cause, such as Leeds Infirmary.

Mr Harper, the local clergyman, presided over an entertainment that was held in March, 1871; he "discharged his duties with much ability and in a goodly manner." Mr Carr read "The Deceitful Lover" and Miss Ellis sang "The Ladder Stile." Then it was back to Mr Carr for an amusing piece, the essence of which was conveyed in the long title – "Watering Milk, or Choking the Best Cow." Mr Wildman rendered two songs and Mr Tiplady spoke. Miss Ellis returned to sing "Barney O'Hea" and "Tapping at the Garden Gate"– and so on until 10pm, for there were many encores. So often did the audience demand more from Mr Wildman and Miss Ellis that they were kept going '"like a barrel organ." A London visitor who attended the entertainment compared it favourably with anything he had seen in the "far city."

In the unlikely setting of a shanty town known as Jerusalem, where space for a public event must have been at a premium, the members of an audience watched with lower jaws drooping in astonishment as a workman carried a hurdy-gurdy about the room and played a polka, "which had a very exciting influence on some of the women, who could not keep their feet still." A contingent from Batty Green attended this concert and had to walk back along the tramway as far as Sebastopol, thence "by the nearest way" to their homes. The worst part of the journey was the crossing of the viaduct leading to the tunnel – a viaduct on which the train bearing the provisions had come to grief – for "there were openings between the sleepers wide enough for a corpulent boniface to drop through. Without a light, the danger would have been imminent…"

In December, 1871, a Reading Room was opened at Denthead, at the sole cost of the Midland, who agreed to maintain a supply of newspapers and periodicals. Mr Duffy, manager of the works on the northern side of Blea Moor Tunnel, presided, being delighted to promote the welfare of the Mission and the Reading Room. Whereupon, the Batty Green Handbellringers closed the meeting with a merry peal.

Above: An impression of Birkett Cutting.
Left and below: As no photographs of navvies at work on the Settle-Carlisle appear to have survived, these pictures of lead-miners of Nenthead are offered as examples of the appearance of the labourers of late Victorian times.

Pay-Day at Batty Green. Much of a navvy's income went on strong drink.

Law and Disorder in the Shanties

EDWARD TOWN travelled from South Wales to Ribblesdale, attracted by the 10s a day he might earn while working on the railway. In 1870, he made his home at Horton and then "wooed and won a fair lady amongst the hills of the north." In October of that year, Edward "led her to the altar at the lead-covered church at Horton." The quotations are from a newspapers account of the Welshman's dastardly deeds. He already had a wife and family when he wed the lass from the Dales. A message from his wife triggered off the events that led to his apprehension. On October 22, a telegram was received by Superintendent of Police Cockshott at Settle, and he forwarded it to Superintendent Exton of Ingleton. He contacted PC Goodison of Gearstones, who received it late on Sunday. The policeman had to wait until just after midnight before he could

legally act; he then "pounced on his unsuspicious prey." The bigamist was taken under police escort to Swansea, where he faced his wife and family. It is related that his new "wife," on being separated from him, wept copiously and pledged that she would never forget him!

When Contract No.1 was negotiated in 1869, the Contractor had to provide police cover as required by the local magistrate. Most of the shanties being on Ingleton Fells, the village of Ingleton had the strongest police presence – Superintendent William Exton, supported by Sergeant William Clapham. At Settle, Superintendent Copeland and PC Plowright (initially) manned the police station. In the "field" were Robert Walker (Horton-in-Ribblesdale), Robert Bold (Garsdale), George Renton (Lea Yeat), Archie Cameron (Batty Green) and John

Above: Jack Foster, the Austwick butcher, is said to have taken meat into North Ribblesdale to sell to the navvies. He is portrayed in a relaxed mood. (Author's collection).

The Contractor's Hotel

Settle and the Railway

Above: The Church and its environments before the Settle-Carlisle was constructed.
Below: A Victorian print features a viaduct and embankments relating to the new line.

Otter Taylor (Denthead). The magistrates, local "big wigs," dealt out sentences with Victorian harshness and often sent a man to prison for a trivial matter. Newspapers were less inhibited than they are today and, for example, did not hesitate to use the words "rogue and vagabond" when a navvy called George Wilson was sentenced to a month in prison for being found in a barn at Dent Head with intent to commit a felony.

Court records are important not just as a catalogue of wrong-doing but because they give an insight into local life. George Morris, in 1870, stole some carpenter's tools from the grocery shop of Mr Burgoyne at Batty Green. The tools belonged to a man who was doing work there and who subsequently met a man carrying one of the tools. He said it had been given to him by someone who was travelling towards Settle. There followed an exciting chase, the pursuers being the grocer and Mr Burgoyne, occupying a horse-drawn trap. About two miles down the dale they caught up with George Morris, who had a jack plane – one of the missing items – in his hands. Morris actually asked for a lift to Settle. "Yes, jump in," said Mr Burgoyne, who turned the horse and trap towards Batty Green and, on arriving at the shanty town, delivered Morris and the jack plane to the police. Morris appeared at Ingleton Court and was sentenced to three months' imprisonment. One of the charges against Morris failed because the chief witness had absconded.

In the case of Policeman Jack (Atkins), the pugilist who delivered the blow that killed Nebby Scandalous one Sunday morning in 1874, the jury at the inquest, which was held at Skipton, returned a verdict of manslaughter against Jack, but no further action could be taken. He had decamped. To be fair to Jack, it had been Nebby who challenged him to a fight that ended after three punishing rounds with the collapse and death of Nebby. Perhaps he had not heard of Jack's record. Less than two years earlier, he had slain a man in fisticuffs and was sent to trial. Jack was then set at liberty – because it was considered he had not long to live.

The Sedbergh Bench sent convicted men to the Wakefield House of Correction, for Sedbergh was then a northern outpost of the West Riding of Yorkshire. In June, 1873, Henry Spring began a term of 21 days of imprisonment for stealing a cloth waistcoat belonging to Richard Bragg, who kept an inn at Denthead. A month later, at Sedbergh, Richard Tippet and John Mutton, navvies, each received a sentence of two months of imprisonment for stealing at Denthead one woollen handkerchief and one cotton handkerchief, value 3s, the property of George Gills, a miner of Denthead. They were alleged to have removed the handkerchiefs from a cabin at Black Moss, adjacent to the Rise Hill railway tunnel, which was then in course of excavation.

Elsewhere, a spade was stolen from Cragg Hill cutting at Horton-in-Ribblesdale and a counterpane from Jericho. Men who tampered with their sub-tickets (issued when they received an advance on their wages) were brought before the court with a wearying regularity. Among them was the aptly-named John Money, a miner at Blea Moor Tunnel. When he applied for 10s the sub-ticket was given to him in the tunnel, yet the ticket produced in court had been made out for 40s. John was committed to the next Assizes, to be held in Leeds.

The few Irishmen among the workforce were exposed to bad feeling on the part of the Englishmen, who were not above threatening the hapless men from the Emerald Isle. Thomas Cooper, a stonemason employed by Mr Duffy, a contractor for bridges, was with some pals in the Crown Inn at Settle on a summer evening In 1870 when he turned to a group of Irishmen and told them they would have to leave the area before noon on the following day. A disturbance took place. Peter Quin, foreman, was in another room; he came and tried to restore order but was struck twice in the face by Thomas Cooper. The police were called and "the row ceased." Cooper was fined 20s, with 12s costs.

.   .   .   .   .

Around Ribblehead

Right: A photograph of the 1870's clearly shows the method of constructing Ribblehead viaduct, using timber framing until the arches had been turned and having steam-operated lifting gear on the gantry (B.R.).
Below: The Horton butcher calls at Salt Lake Cottages early this century.
Below, right: Partly-completed Long Meg, or Eden Lacy, which spans the Eden.

Above: Saturday night at Batty Green. *Below:* Station Inn, Ribblehead.

Under the Influence of John Barleycorn

AN EXCISE OFFICER, John Barwise, pressed the Sedbergh Bench to impose a heavy penalty in a case where a man was accused of selling beer without a license "on account of the quantity of excisable liquor which is illegally sold by the hut-keepers on the new line of railway." A quaint name for strong drink was "John Barleycorn." It was generally recognised that the ale-can was responsible for most of the crimes. "Drink has been a gigantic hindrance," was one sorrowful comment. An outrageous example was when an inebriated navvy threw some dynamite charges on to the fire at Gearstones.

Temperance workers were concerned that two public houses, one of them being also a brewery, stood quite near the pay office at Batty Green. The Settle Temperance Society held meetings at which everyone was urged to "sign the pledge." Some did, at the time, while those who were shy of displaying their feelings in public later visited Mr Tiplady, the railway missionary, and signed in private. A solitary voice raised against the temperance movement was heard to say that its supporters crammed everything down men's throats save drink!

James Mathers' "Welcome Home" at Batty Green was a licensed drinking place. Poor James died at Ingleton under the wheels of his wagon when trying to stop a bolting horse.

The "Junction Inn" at Garsdale became notorious for lawlessness under Emmanuel Brammall. Most hardened drinkers indulged themselves in private, frequenting one of the huts. The few excise officers skulked about the camps, peering in windows or, if they were not well-known, hoping when visiting a hut to be offered drink by someone who would then accept payment for it.

Drinking led to brawling, or even to pitched battles between rival groups. Two strong navvies who agreed to a bare-fisted fight had not been fighting long when one of the backers success-fully appealed for the conflict to be postponed so that his man could sober up. The fight was re-commenced early next day – and was over by 5.30am. A navvy who had been drinking at the "Welcome Home" staggered forth and found the tramway was a relatively dry spot on which to sleep off his condition. The following morning, the recumbent man was decapitated by the first train. Peter Miles, a mason, drank hard and long at the "Railway Inn," at Batty Green. He set off for Sebastopol but was overtaken by fatigue and fell asleep on the tramway. The guard of an engine returning from Jericho told an inquest that when the engine was about 150 yards from Batty Green platform, a jerk was felt. He ordered the driver to stop the locomotive and found the body of Miles. The dead man was 30 years old and a native of Bootle.

The career of Emmanuel Bramall had more ups and downs than a Pennine road. Garsdale is a little to the north of the area that concerns us in this booklet, yet Emmanuel was such a character that his inclusion will add considerably to its authentic flavour. In 1870, he was a labourer who had hopes of entering the drinks trade. He was fined 30s for selling ale without a license. In many subsequent court cases, his name was spelt in various ways, which did not matter, for he was generally known as Nobby and was sometimes referred to as such. In February, 1873, Nobby was fined 20s with 13s costs for selling beer at the "Junction Inn" outside licensing hours. PC Bold found 18 men in the place; he watched the landlady bring in a quart of beer, which was paid for in his presence. Nobby unwisely obstructed PC Bold by holding a door and preventing the constable from passing through it. An additional fine of 1s was imposed, together with 8s 6d costs.

In June of the same year, PC Inman visited Nobby's premises at about 8.15am and discovered 16 or 17 men, several of whom were "the worse for drink." Nobby was subsequently fined for permitting drunkenness in the house. The notorious landlord had a wife with a roving eye. It eventually rested on a labourer called Samuel Seely, who lodged at the inn. She left Nobby in the autumn of 1874, and her husband went to Wales looking for her, leaving Seely in the house. When Nobby returned, Seely had gone and with him a black silk handkerchief, a navvy's slop and a boy's suit of clothes. The man was tracked down in Fifeshire. The missing objects were in his possession. He had been living with Nobby's wife for three weeks, but by then she had left him and gone to North Shields. At the court hearing, to everyone's surprise, Seely was acquitted.

Nobby's career continued ingloriously almost to the end of "navvy time." In March, 1875, he was charged with an assault upon Elizabeth Thompson. He was at this time the owner of the "Junction Inn," with William Thompson as his tenant, Elizabeth being his daughter. She was fetching water for the use of the house when Nobby, without provocation, struck her on the eye. That was the tale told at Sedbergh Petty Sessions by William Thompson. The magistrates believed Nobby when he said that Thompson was drunk in the middle of the day and that he had turned out all the people including his daughter. He had given her a black eye two or three hours before the alleged assault took place. The case against Nobby was dismissed and so, whatever his faults, he was proved to be chival-

Gearstones, near Ribblehead.

rous towards a lady. The reporter attending Sedbergh Court noted that this lady was a "showily dressed girl!"

The Gearstones Inn, which stood beside the turnpike road near Ribblehead, secured a place in local folklore when young Sharland the engineer, and some of his men, stayed here while surveying the line. A sudden blizzard marooned them. Eventually they had to tunnel out of the inn so that they could obtain water from a trough. The enduring fame of Gearstones was ensured in May, 1873, when a railway labourer called George Young caused an explosion by tossing some caps and a portion of "Nobel's patent safety powder dynamite" on to the fire. The inn-keeper, Francis Yates, and his daughter Alice, were on the premises when Young arrived between 4pm and 5pm and demanded a drink. An hour later, Yates was seen to have a tin box in his hand. In the box were objects like gun caps, but longer.

Alice Yates heard him say that he would not strike one of the caps for a sovereign, or the house would be blown up. At about 7pm, her worst fears were realised when she heard a loud report and the house was so shaken by the blast she thought it would collapse. The kitchen and lobby filled with smoke. At the time of the explosion, there were 13 people in the house and seven in the kitchen where Yates had been drinking. At the court hearing, John Butcher related that he had seen Young take a tin box from his pocket; he removed something from the box – which Butcher had taken to be tobacco – and threw it on the fire. A loud explosion followed.

Yates left the house. Butcher, who was described as "a navvy on the tramp," followed him on to the road, "collared him and knocked him down." Butcher dragged the hapless man into the inn and stood guard over him until PC Cameron arrived. The accused was found to have 19s 6d, a tobacco box, a knife, a box of caps and a portion of Nobel's patent safety powder dynamite. He was committed to the Assizes. The damage to the inn was less serious than might be supposed. The oven and fireplace grate were blown out of their places, 15 panes of glass were broken, also part of a window frame and a clock. The blast shattered the glass in a framed funeral card!

An Evening to Remember

A writer in an issue of "Chambers's Journal" of 1873 described his visit to the hut of the Pollen family and the high spirits of the family and their navvy lodgers when a party was organised.

ENTER a stalwart navvy, whose powerful frame contrasted comically with his shamefaced countenance. He was blushing from ear to ear, yet there was a twinkle in the big black eye of the goodlooking fellow. He bore a message from the navvy brotherhood in the other room. He craved humbly of Mother Pollen that he and they should be admitted to participate in the festivities of the evening…

Pollen pronounced at once for their admission. Mrs Pollen only stipulated for order; and the navvies trooped solemnly in and seated themselves on the extreme edge of a form. Mrs Pollen helped them to wine, of which all ceremoniously partook; and then the black-eyed navvy took Mrs Pollen aside, an interview which resulted in the introduction of a pail of strong ale and a bottle of whisky. The navvies were a decided acquisition. First, the black-eyed navvy played a lively spring on his fiddle… Then Tom Purgin sang "My Pretty Jane."

A dance followed – something between a reel and an Irish jig – in which the black-eyed navvy immensely distinguished himself by playing and dancing at the same time… The beer-pail was replenished, the ladies were radiant with good-humour and enjoyment, the navvies were making themselves as agreeable as possible, and the evening altogether was passing most hilariously…

Cases of illicit drinking came before the magistrates with a wearying monotony. One could understand the navvies in a bleak area like Blea Moor becoming hard drinkers, but cases were reported from the Lowland areas, too. In 1871, George Askell was fined £5 for selling beer without a licence in huts at Stainforth. Richard Buckle was fined £3.3s (also costs totalling £1.17s) for selling beer at Horton without troubling the Excise authorities. The market town of Settle had inns in abundance but navvies still found the back-street drinking places.

In March, 1874, Superintendent Copeland, of Settle Police, received a number of complaints about illicit drinking and he thus gave a pep-talk to his men, one of whom, PC Plowright, assumed a disguise and visited the home of John Duggan, a railway labourer living in Upper Settle. The policeman was served with a pint of beer and Duggan was handed sixpence and gave three-pence back in change. At court, Duggan pleaded guilty and was sent to prison for three weeks. Thomas Smith, a labourer who lived at Stainforth, called at the "Royal Oak" in Settle, drank too much and appears to have mistaken the road when he left. He fell into the Ribble near King's Mill and was found drowned.

John Barwise and Joseph Wilson, the Excise officers for Sedbergh and Bentham respectively, were known to prowl around huts at night and, if they were not well-known in a locality, to enter a hut and ask for beer. One such hut entered by Wilson stood near the southern end of Blea Moor tunnel. James Oxendale, who lived in the Railway Huts at Dent Head, was fined 20s with costs for selling beer without a licence, though evidence was given that the chief witness for the prosecution – a navvy named Pugh – had a grievance against Oxendale, having been turned out of his lodgings by Oxendale's wife.

The navvies must not be allowed to become too friendly with John Barleycorn.

At the "Welcome Home"

MRS MATHERS, who presided over the "Welcome Home", an inn at Batty Green, would also—if asked—advance money on goods left with her. In most cases, the money was promptly spent on ale. This happened in June, 1872, when Benjamin Higgins (a tall man) and James Jackson (a diminutive man) pawned a bundle containing a shirt, a flannel singlet and two handkerchiefs, receiving two shillings.

The two men had been working on the line at Horton and now had jobs at Batty Green. They visited the "Welcome Home" for lodgings, but were unsuccessful. They spun a hard-luck story and managed to pawn some of their property, promptly buying a quart of beer and three pennorth of bread.

On the following morning, they were back at the inn, relating to one Henry Myers, who lodged at the inn, that they had slept in the open. Myers, feeling sorry for them, handed over fourpence in copper and two quarts of ale. He then went to lie, fully clothed on his bed and fell asleep. The two men repaid his generosity by emptying his pockets. They took three 2s pieces, two halfcrowns, thruppence in copper, a razor and case, pocket knife, an ounce of tobacco and a box of matches.

Mrs Mather's daughter had seen Higgins with a handful of silver and PC Cameron was informed. He soon apprehended the two men, recovering the goods and the money with the exception of 4s.3d, which – in short time – the men had converted into liquid assets.

The Bench sentenced each man to three months' imprison-ment, with hard labour.

From a newspaper report on Batty Green, July, 1874:

"The navvies have often to be domiciled on wild moorlands, far away from towns and villages. Some of these heath-clad moors are so wild and so shut out from everything that can contribute to the enjoyment of life, that it is difficult to keep these men for any length of time at one place… Navvies are often rude in language to one another, but to missionaries or strangers who wish to do them good they are generally respectful. Kind words and deeds are sure to meet with their respect."

A REPORT on the consecration of additional burying ground at Chapel-le-Dale, August 12, 1871:

On account of the terrible havoc made amongst the inhabitants at the new railway works on Blea Moor by the smallpox, the burial ground had become quite too small as the resting place of the dead. When it is stated that nearly 60 persons since last July but one have been interred in the small burial ground attached to that small but neat house of prayer, anyone who knows the place will see that the additional accommodation for the dead has not been made too soon. Over 30 persons who have died in the smallpox lie in the old burial ground. Upon an average, before the railway works were commenced, there were about two interments per year... Earl Bective has kindly given the new ground. To unite both portions of ground, the old road to the farms which lie at the foot of Whernside has been broken up and a new and better road made. All the farmers who travelled over the road to their farmsteads, like sensible men, gave their willing consent to the alteration. Monday last being the day appointed for consecrating the new ground. Dr Ryan, vicar of Bradford and lately a colonial bishop, attended in place of the Bishop of Ripon to perform the site of consecration.

This covered wagon served as an ambulance.

Matters of Life and Death

THE FIRST AMBULANCE at Batty Green was horse-drawn, of course, and resembled one of the "covered wagons" made famous by their use on the plains of the American West. The Yorkshire type of wagon took patients to a temporary wooden structure. Alfred Johnson was admitted in a hurry on January 6, 1871. Alfred had damaged a leg while working in the cutting at Helwith Bridge and the leg was amputated below the knee by Drs Green and Hartley. Money for medical attention came in part from a Settle and Carlisle Sick Fund, established among the work people towards the end of 1870, there being 140 members by the spring of 1873. A shortfall in funds was met by organising an entertainment in the Settle Music Hall, over £10 being raised.

When the Midland Railway Company took over Mr Ashwell's Contract – he was in financial difficulty – they maintained their own doctor at a fine new hospital that was constructed at Batty Green. Dr Swain, of Sedbergh, was summoned when there was an accident or ill-health at Dent Head.

Doctors were not themselves immune from misfortune. In the summer of 1871, during a thunderstorm, Dr Griffiths set off from Batty Green to Ingleton, where his professional services were needed. A young man had been thrown from a horse, injuring his head. The doctor's horse, startled by a flash of lightning, reared up, the rider being thrown to the ground. Happily, he was able to remount and to resume his journey.

In its first year of operation, the narrow gauge railway from Batty Green to Blea Moor claimed several lives. Gloom descended on the shanty towns when the news spread of the death of Annie Wall, aged 7. She had arrived at Ingleton station with her aunt, Mrs Powell, and they travelled through Chapel-le-Dale and lodged at Sebastopol. Shortly before noon, the train journey began. Mr Powell, having met his wife and their young relative, helped them into the wagons, Mrs Powell and Annie occupying the first of three and Mr Powell entering the last. Near Underhill's cutting, and not far short of a temporary bridge, the locomotive left the track. Annie was buried with muck and scalded by hot water from the boiler, Mrs Powell being scalded about her legs. Her husband was uninjured. The driver of the locomotive suffered bruising. The fireman, who leapt off, was uninjured. At the inquest, the Coroner returned a verdict of "accidental death."

At an inquest held in October, 1870, into the death of a man at Pavilion Cottages, near the Stone House, in the upper valley of the Dee, the Coroner heard that George Hodge, aged 63, had fallen into a cellar being constructed to hold the stock of Mr W.M. Boden, grocer and innkeeper. A verdict of accidental death was returned. Some men died of terrible injuries without the ministrations of a doctor, and one such was James Sherman, driver at Blea Moor Tunnel. He was bringing a horse-drawn wagon out of the tunnel one evening when he was knocked down. One of the wheels ran over his ankle, crushing it badly. Sherman was lifted on to a cart and conveyed to his lodgings at Batty Green, a journey of five miles. When his hut was reached, he had lost so much blood it was trickling from the back of the cart. Sherman refused medical help and died soon afterwards, the Coroner at the inquest returning a verdict of "Accidental death." John

Lee, who fell off a wagon and went under the train on the tramway, lost his left arm and leg. He was taken to his lodgings at Sebastopol and died four hours later.

In February, 1873, one of the legs of a crane being used in Langcliffe cutting fell on young John Owen, who was instantly killed. The inquest verdict was "Accidental death" but the Coroner recommended that in future all cranes used on the line should undergo an inspection daily, by some competent person in the employ of the company. Owen's sorrowing mates attended the funeral at Settle parish church. A tombstone was raised to mark his grave. Following the inscription is a quotation in Welsh.

In the dusty recesses of Blea Moor Tunnel, in October, 1874, Henry Cartwright, aged 23, was at work when he was struck by some falling rock and died instantly. His body was reverently borne to the school at Dent Head and lay here until the inquest could be held. Miners had an almost cheerful disregard for safety measures connected with dynamite. Unexploded dynamite was left in holes in the rocks, when it should have been removed in case it was struck by a driller who did not know it was there. In May, 1874, John Roberts and Caleb James – the latter known as Birmingham Bill – were drilling when old dynamite exploded. Bill died soon afterwards; the other man lost an eye and had the sight in the other eye greatly impaired.

From the Burial Register of the church in Mallerstang.

Above: Sub contractor's grave, Chapel-le-Dale.

BURIALS in the Parish of *Chapel le Dale or Ingleton Fells* in the County of *York* in the Year 1871				
Name.	Abode.	When buried.	Age.	By whom the Ceremony was performed.
William Dean No. 233.	Sebastopool	Jan. 22	11 month	Wm Harper
John Hollerenshaw No. 234.	Sebastopool	Jan. 24	40 years	Wm Harper
Charles Bibby No. 235.	Sebastopool	Jan. 31	9 month	Wm Harper
Louisa Annie Thompson No. 236.	Jerico Lo	Feb. 1	3 years	Wm Harper
Fredrick Little No. 237.	Inkerman	Feb. 5	4 years	Wm Harper
Tom Atkinson Little No. 238.	Inkerman	Feb. 9	1 year & six month	Wm Harper
Thomas Smith No. 239.	Jericho	Feb. 12	10 month	Wm Harper

Rest in Peace

Left: This page from the burial register at Chapel-le-Dale includes among the places of "abode" the shanties of Sebastopol and Inkerman, both familiar through frequent mention in the Crimean War, when railway navvies, working hard, laid a railway from the main port to the front line. Some of these men had perhaps arrived to work on the Settle-Carlisle, the last of the major lines to be built by the traditionally large number of workers.

On another day, Henry Wright died when the drill he was using connected with some dynamite. Henry lingered for a while in Batty Green hospital. After the inquest, held at the "Welcome Home," many of his friends followed the coffin to the last resting place in Chapel-le-Dale. John Thompson was drying off dynamite at a brazier in Blea Moor Tunnel, one April day in 1875, when the dynamite exploded and he died instantly. Thompson was 28 years of age and his body was interred in the yard of Chapel-le-Dale.

In the spring and summer of 1871, smallpox was detected in the hutments on and around Batty Green. It was, according to a newspaper reporter, "painfully prevalent" at Sebastopol and Jericho. Five funerals of victims had been held in a single week, and from a single hut at Sebastopol were carried the bodies of a mother and three children. At a meeting held in the National School at Ingleton, on March 22, 1871, consideration was given to the enlargement of the burial ground.

Meanwhile, when smallpox began to wreak "terrible havoc amongst the inhabitants at the new railway works on Blea Moor," the necessity of providing isolation facilities was an urgent consideration. At Batty Green, the contractor erected two huts for the accommodation of 10 patients. In due course, a covered way and another building 48 feet long, were provided. It was now possible to accommodate a total of 20 patients. Patients' clothes were "baked" in a large oven and all washing and disinfecting of garments were undertaken on the premises. The hospital was managed by Mr and Mrs Halifax.

By June, it was reported that no death had occurred at Batty Green for a fortnight, and that those who had caught the disease, having been

removed to the hospital, were responding to medical attention and good nursing. They had "yielded to the remedies employed." Soon afterwards, an upsurge in the number of cases led to four more deaths – two of children at Jericho and two of men who had been moved to the hospital.

In July, the medical workers were disheartened by a resurgence of smallpox. The inhabitants of the shanty towns were being urged to be more hygienic. The interiors of yet more huts were whitewashed. At the hospital, washing and disinfecting were being done on the premises. A "dead house" awaited those who could not fight the disease, and the convalescents were provided with a small library. By July 10, 35 cases had been admitted to the hospital. Of these, 19 were cured and released and 13 remained.

Minimus, the pen-name of a local ratepayer, had little doubt about how to deal with the smallpox outbreak at Batty Green. He wrote to the "Lancaster Guardian" asserting that much of the trouble was caused by intemperance. Furthermore, all above the age of 14 should be vaccinated. "The ratepayers of the township in which Batty Green is situated should call a vestry and appoint an 'officer for the suppression of nuisances'." The remarks of Minimus were quietly and painstakingly answered by the Medical Officer, Edwin S. Green.

Many people had a dread of going near Batty Green during that smallpox summer, yet in July a party of Settle people went ahead with their plans to visit the dalehead railway works. A newspaper writer was impressed by the daring deeds of a young lady who, "with less fear than the rest and with a love for adventure, in spite of loving and fervent entreaties from her lady companions, mounted the locomotive and started on the tramway for the tunnel. This feat, which was considered too daring for the rest of the party, was only the prelude to further deeds of adventure. After being properly attired for the feat she had undertaken, she descended in succession the three shafts of the tunnel..."

A strange story concerning the Batty Green hospital was published in a local newspaper in 1874. After asserting that the navvy, when drunk, was not too fussy about his bed, and that this might consist of the roadside, the moor, a wet ditch – or a coffin – the newspaper reporter mentioned a visit to the navvy's hospital by some gentlemen who toured the wards with interest and then entered the "deadhouse." One of the party lifted the lid of a new coffin and was startled to find it was already occupied.

He reported there was a man in the coffin, whereupon another member of the party suggested the authorities had forgotten to bury him. "No,'" said the one who had lifted the lid. "He has his clothes on." The lid was lifted again and there lay a man, fully clothed, his trousers stained with blood. Had he been murdered? Had the murderer brought the body to this building by night, slipping it in the coffin? The visitors discussed the strange happening and concluded that the coroner must be informed. All this time the "murdered" man lay face down in the coffin. A third man approached the coffin and pinched the man's left leg to feel whether it was rigid or flabby. The "corpse" raised his head and said: "Can't you let a poor fellow sleep quietly!"

The men helped him out of the coffin, telling the navvy he was lucky, and might well have been buried alive. The navvy, though still quite drunk, promptly asked for thruppence so that he might get another pint of beer. He did not seem particularly worried when he discovered the coffin was used for the reception of people suffering from smallpox and fevers. When his legs were steady, the navvy left Batty Green, travelling in the direction of Keighley.

An addition to the burial ground in Chapel-le-Dale was consecrated by the aforementioned Dr Ryan, "vicar of Bradford," on August 12, 1871. It was stated that 30 persons had been interred in the old yard since the smallpox epidemic occurred. On average, before the railway works began, there were two interments a year. Sixty interments had taken place during the past year. Earl Bective gave the land, and the farmers co-operated by donating land when a new stretch of road was required. The day of consecration was hot and sunny – perfect hay-making weather after a wet season – and the congregation was "as good as could be expected." The Revd E. Smith had the spiritual supervision of the dale when the churchyard extension was consecrated.

Some curious tales were related of funerals at Chapel-le-Dale. Carrying a coffin from huts on Blea Moor could be hard and thirsty work, and on one occasion the bearers decided to have a drink at the "Hill Inn." For a time, the coffin was left in the road. The saddest story concerned the twin daughters of a miner living in the Tunnel Huts,

Above: Blea Moor, the best-known of the Settle-Carlisle signal boxes. The first box was built beside the "down" line.

Below: Denthead viaduct under construction. The image was reversed.

Blea Moor; they died as infants in December, 1871. Notice of the funeral was given to the curate in charge of the parish in the absence of the Revd E. Smith. The funeral cortege arrived about five minutes before the appointed time, which was 2pm. Yet no bell was heard tolling, neither were parson and sexton in sight. Then the parson made his appearance and told the bereaved parents he had forgotten about the funeral. Consequently, he had not instructed the sexton to make a grave. The sorrowing father borrowed some implements, dug a grave, tolled the bell and, when the short service was over, filled in the grave.

A visitor to Batty Green in the autumn of 1871 arrived just in time to see the funeral of a young man from Tunnel Huts. The coffin was taken to the tramway, where a locomotive and single wagon were ready to convey the body down to Batty Green. When Job Hirst, subcontractor on Ribblehead viaduct, died in December, 1872, a committee of workmen and others raised over £43 to purchase a tombstone with which to adorn his grave in the yard of Chapel-le-Dale Church.

Visiting Batty Green in 1873, and subsequently describing his experiences in "Chambers's Journal," a writer mentioned a man who could recall a good many deaths at the railway works – deaths from "accidents, low fevers, smallpox, and so on." He had buried "three o' my own." He was "arter a sort the undertaker o' the place. You passed the little church down at Chapel-le-Dale, near the head of the Valley. Well, in the three years, I've toted over a hundred of us down the hill to the little churchyard lying round the church. T'other day I had toted one poor fellow down – he were hale and hearty on Thursday, and on Tuesday he were dead o' eroinsipalis; and I says to the clerk as how I thought I had toted nigh on a hundred over the beck to Chapel-a-Dale. He goes, and has a look at his books, and comes out and says, says he: 'Joe, you've fetched to t'kirkyawd xackly a hundred and ten corps!' I knowed I warn't far out. They've had to add a piece on to t'churchyawd, for it were chock-full'."

When Henry Bachelor was buried here in 1875, it was said that this was the 210th interment. "Now there is some fear that it may have to be enlarged again," wrote the local correspondent. "Two hundred and ten funerals is almost as many, if not quite, as took place in the Chapelry in a hundred years previous to the commencement of the railway works. It is singular that in a mountainous district, so remote from the great centres of industry, men, women and children, from every county in England, as well as from Wales, Scotland and Ireland, should be buried in a quiet churchyard which few of them had heard of before they came into the district. Beneath the shadows of Ingleborough and Whernside, and in one of the loveliest glens in the north of England, many a wanderer from his home and friends has found a quiet resting-place."

Chapel-le-Dale.

Settle-Carlisle Snapshots

Above: Two personalities of the construction period.
William Crackanthorpe, of Newbiggin Hall, asked a surveying party to spare one tree from a favourite wood – so that he might hang Midland men from it! Mr Sharland, the young Tasmanian engineer, walked the route the railway would take and was marooned with his men in Gearstones when an unexpected blizzard occurred .

Left: Settle station, at the start of the 1914-18 war, when volunteers assembled to go off to war. A group of such men is pictured below.

Settle Station was built mainly with stone brought from the quarries of the Bradford district. Water for the buildings and also for locomotives flowed in a lineside channel, and the Midland paid a local farmer for the supply. If they were late with payment, the farmer diverted the water. A railway employee was soon sent to the farm with the money.

Above: Newly completed viaduct at Settle.

Below: Signal box at Crosby Garrett.

A locomotive almost covered by snow.

High Arches at Ribblehead

RIBBLEHEAD VIADUCT, an ageing giant in blue limestone, presides over moor and bog where the Settle-Carlisle takes to the hills. With 24 arches and a maximum height of about 100 feet – certainly not the 165 feet that is frequently quoted – Ribblehead is the largest and best-known structure, testifying to Victorian self-confidence. Years ago, it was a symbol of defiance in the verbal tussle between British Rail and 22,265 people who objected in writing when the closure was announced. A dog qualified as a "user" and its jubilant owner sent along its pawprint!

The viaduct might also be thought of as a memorial to those who worked on the viaduct and tunnel, between Ribblehead and Dent Head. It was for them that the shanty towns were erected. When the construction of the line ended, the men dispersed, the huts were demolished and sold and all but the heaps of defective bricks were blown away by the Pennine storms.

Ribblehead viaduct is not straight. It has to curve gently towards Blea Moor. It presents a large but strong outline to the westerly gales that are funnelled by Chapel-le-Dale.

The men who designed and built the viaduct must have felt over-awed in the presence of

Ribblehead Viaduct: where the Settle-Carlisle crosses Batty Green on its way
to the high hills (photo: Peter Fox).

Whernside (2,414ft). Shafts were dug through peat and clay to reach bedrock. A fanciful story is told that the piers were "built on wool," which may be an illusion to money the Midland directors raised among the Bradford woolmen. In fact, the bases of the piers were set in concrete. The engineers lacked the experience and confidence to make the entire structure of concrete, though in a few years "Cement Bobby" Macalpine would be operating his cement-mixer and turning out concrete viaducts in Scotland; he was responsible for Glenfinnan, on the line to Mallaig.

Ribblehead contains over 30,000 cubic yards of limestone. It arose behind a framework of wooden staging. The weather was atrocious. In 1870, John Crossley, the Midland's Chief Engineer, reported that the staging was in position and that "Good weather and men alone are wanted." Every sixth pier was made thicker than the others so that if one pier were to fall it would take only five piers with it.

The exact number of arches was not determined until two years after the laying of the first stone. Crossley had to balance the numbers of available masons and earthworkers. He deployed men to the best advantage. Welsh masons were preferred – and in March, 1872, they struck for better wages. The outcome of this industrial dispute is not known, but the masons were "out" for over a week.

The arches of Ribblehead were lined with one and a-half million bricks, being a mixture of local shale and clay baked in 10 ovens that were built a few yards from where the viaduct was taking shape. The production rose to 20,000 bricks a day and it is related that when they were tossed from the kilns they "rang like pots." These bricks were soon replaced

Those of us who suffer from Settle-Carlisleitis were alarmed to be told by British Rail in 1981 that this famous structure was deteriorating to such an extent it would have to be

Opposite page: Dent Head viaduct, from the Land Plan.

Below: A view of the partly-completed Ribblehead viaduct from the east.

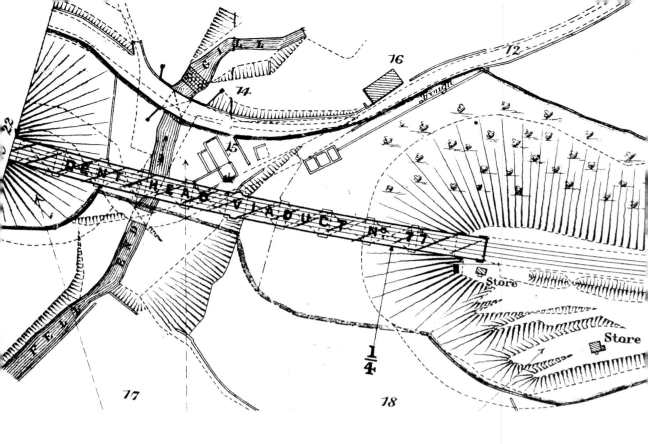

replaced within as little as five years – or the line must be closed. At the time of the BR report, a cost of £6m for remedial work was mentioned (the estimated cost is now between £2.4m and £4m). At close quarters, it certainly looked careworn. Notices with white lettering on a red background warned all but the employees of British Rail to stay clear. Ribblehead is in one of the draughtiest places in England. A maintenance man told me of days when planks on the scaffolding went "up and down like piano keys."

Rain, not the notorious gales, caused the major damage to Ribblehead. Water seeping through the slate and asphalt laid at the time of construction found its way into the piers, mixing with the "fill," the mortar and rubble, and reducing it to a sort of clayey mud. Water eventually trickled through the outer skin from cracks between the blocks of limestone, having washed away the mortar. Limestone has no bedding grain and when compressed – as when the mortar is washed away – it is easily shattered.

Yet the viaduct epitomises the spirit of the Settle-Carlisle railway. "You have to take your hat off to the builders," I was told by an engineer. "When you consider the primitive equipment they had, it is a fantastic piece of engineering work." The railway was "singled" over Ribblehead viaduct in 1984. Sophisticated equipment controls the traffic. The viaduct was restored at a cost of several million pounds.

I stood at Ribblehead on a wintry day in 1978 when steam returned to the Settle-Carlisle after 10 years. The "Green Arrow" appeared, speeding towards the viaduct. I would have preferred a Midland locomotive, proudly wearing its coat of "Derby red" but none was available at that time. I stood, along with Mr Bannister, the last surviving member of Sir Nigel's loco design team, and we watched the train sweep by, being little more than a smudge against the swirling vapour.

When the mist comes down from Whernside, enveloping Batty Green in a damp shroud, my imagination people's this wild landscape with the old navvy throng.

.   .   .   .   .

An Epilogue

IN THE EARLY part of 1875, the rateable value of the huts on Contract No.1 was £600 and it was stated that the rates would diminish daily as buildings were removed on completion of the major works. Down at Settle, "the progress of railway works in the vicinity has already more or less disturbed the former repose of its streets, and ere long the place will be further enlivened by the arrival and departure of trains at a commodious new station… Well-built cottages are already springing up in the immediate neighbourhood of the new station, and still further improvements may no doubt be looked for, in keeping with the spirit of the times."

The first goods train travelled from Carlisle to Settle in August and subsequently the freight traffic bedded down the line as masons completed the stations and other buildings. By September, "many of the huts on the moor at Batty Green have been removed and many of the working people have left. It speaks well for the (remaining) railway population that they require only one policeman, PC Walker, to look after them." He ranged from Horton to Dent Head, "over 10 miles, through a very wild and hilly country."

A visitor to Dent Head in October watched men pulling down empty huts. The plan was to take down the outlying shanties and to maintain Batty Green as a workplace and dormitory until the last moment. "The men who have to go some distance on the line to their work are conveyed to and fro by an engine… Between Batty Green and Selside, a large number of men are at work making a new road. On the south side of Selside are built a number of model cottages for workmen."

The first passenger train, its engine in dark green livery, hauling carriages with upholstered seats (a new luxury for the third-class passengers), used the line on May 1, 1876 and confirmed man's dominance of a wild countryside when it covered the 86¾ miles between Skipton and Carlisle in 2 hours 5 minutes. Over a century of Pennine weather has confirmed the quality of workmanship. So impermanent are shanty towns, and so vague is folk memory, that it is a major effort to piece together the story of a small army of workmen, their wives and children, who occupied the hutments between Ribblehead and Dent Head.

Those homes were built, used and dismantled in seven brief but turbulent years.

An overcrowded Settle station.

Above: Near Ribblehead Viaduct. Shepherd framed by water crane.

In Memoriam

Opposite: Chapel-le-Dale Church.

Below right: Gravestone in Settle Churchyard to a young Welshman who died in Langcliffe cutting.

Below left: Memorial in Chapel-le-Dale.

TO THE MEMORY
OF THOSE,
WHO THROUGH ACCIDENTS
LOST THEIR LIVES,
IN CONSTRUCTING THE
RAILWAY WORKS,
BETWEEN SETTLE, AND DENT HEAD.

THIS TABLET WAS ERECTED.
AT THE JOINT EXPENSE,
OF THEIR FELLOW WORKMEN,
AND THE
MIDLAND RAILWAY COMPANY.
1869 TO 1876.

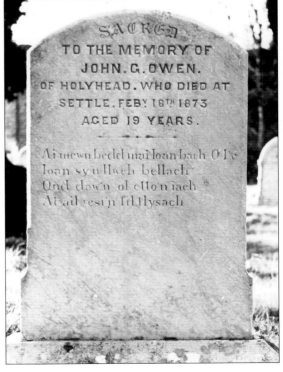

SACRED
TO THE MEMORY OF
JOHN. G. OWEN.
OF HOLYHEAD. WHO DIED AT
SETTLE. FEBY 18TH 1873
AGED 19 YEARS.

Ai mewn bedel mai Ioan bach O I'c
Ioan sy wllach bellach
Ond dawn ol etton iach
At ail resi n fid llysach